GOODBYE

Anxiety

A 31 day devotional
for women of all ages

This book was created with a few people in mind: my friends Cassidy and Emma, my little sister Sara, and especially my 8th grade girls at GVCS.

Introduction

Welcome! You've probably picked up this book because you are all too familiar with the word "anxiety." Maybe you've always struggled with worry, or maybe you're experiencing a stressful stage of life. Whatever the cause may be, you just want your anxiety to go away. I feel for you! I pray that you find peace and comfort throughout the course of this month-long devotional!

Each day revolves around a new Scripture passage that deals with anxiety. You'll begin each devotional by writing out your current anxieties (there is a certain comfort in physically processing your worries and fears). Each scripture is accompanied by a brief paragraph of explanation. It's then your job to apply the verse to your life! Write out the ways you can say goodbye to anxiety, then talk to God!

Philippians 4:4-13

What are you worried about today?

_____

_____

_____

_____

Paul is urging the church to rejoice in their blessings from God. We are called to thankfulness and contentment instead of worry or anxiety. The secret to a stress-free life, Paul says, is to be content in all circumstances.

What do you have to be thankful for? How can you rejoice in your blessings?

_____

_____

_____

_____

_____

Talk to God! Thank him for your blessings and give him your anxieties!

_____

_____

_____

_____

DAY 2

Psalm 94:18-19

What are you worried about today?

_____

_____

_____

_____

Can you relate to David's words, "My foot is slipping?" I know I can! When anxiety consumes us, it often feels as though we are slipping off the edge of a cliff. But, take heart! I have great news! The Lord will support you and keep you from falling. He will comfort you and bring you great joy.

How has the Lord supported you and kept you from falling? Or, how will you allow him to?

_____

_____

_____

_____

_____

Talk to God! Ask him to support you and keep your feet from slipping!

_____

_____

_____

_____

2 Corinthians 12:9-11

What are you worried about today?

_____

_____

_____

_____

Anxiety makes us weak and weary. Lucky for us, God is not weighed down by anxiety. When we are too weak to fight, God steps in and fights for us. He remains perfect in our weakness. So, rejoice! You don't have to fight off your anxiety alone, God will fight it for you.

How has anxiety made you weak and weary?
Will you allow God to step in and fight?

_____

_____

_____

_____

_____

Talk to God! Tell him how you're weak and
ask him to be strong.

_____

_____

_____

_____

DAY 4

Joshua 1:5-9

What are you worried about today?

_____

_____

_____

_____

"Be strong and courageous" is easier said than done. Anxiety weighs down our hearts and makes strength and courage seem impossible. We are blessed to have a God who is our strength and courage. He is with us in every situation, and especially in every worry. Pick yourself up, stand tall, and allow God's strength and courage to lead you.

Do you need strength and courage? What is preventing you from being courageous?

_____

_____

_____

_____

_____

Talk to God! As him to be with you and bring courage wherever you go!

_____

_____

_____

_____

Matthew 6:25-34

What are you worried about today?

_____

_____

_____

_____

The phrase "do not worry" came straight out of the mouth of Jesus! He assures us that our Heavenly Father cares for us. If he cares for simple sparrows, he should care for us a great deal more! He provides for us just as he provides for the rest of his creation; all we have to do is seek his provision.

How has the Lord provided for you? How will you continue to seek God's provision?

_____

_____

_____

_____

_____

Talk to God! Ask him to continue to care for and provide for you.

_____

_____

_____

_____

DAY 6

2 Timothy 1:7

What are you worried about today?

_____

_____

_____

_____

Anxiety, at its core, is fear. You may fear rejection, fear discomfort, or fear disappointment. Whatever you fear, anxiety won't let you forget it. We have to remember that fear does not come from God, nor does anything unrighteous. Instead of focusing on what isn't of God, focus on what IS of God: power, love, and self-discipline.

What fears are causing you anxiety? How can you let go of those fears?

_____

_____

_____

_____

_____

Talk to God! Ask him to give you a spirit of power, love, and self discipline.

_____

_____

_____

_____

Jeremiah 29:11-14a

What are you worried about today?

_____

_____

_____

_____

Isn't it great to know that our paths have already been marked? The Lord has a plan for you, and even better, it's a plan of hope! We can call on the Lord in times of trouble and he will listen. He will assure us of the path ahead: a path full of hope and an ordained future.

Are you calling on the Lord in times of anxiety?
Do you have faith in the hope ahead?

_____

_____

_____

_____

Talk to God! Call on him for help and thank
him for the plan he created for you!

_____

_____

_____

_____

DAY 8

Jeremiah 17:5-8

What are you worried about today?

_____

_____

_____

_____

Anxiety takes a hold of us when we trust in
human ability. When we rely on the strength of
our own human nature, we fail; human
strength is temporary. When we trust in God's
divine ability, we are invincible; God's strength
is eternal. Once we can trust in God's ability to
take care of our worries, fear will vanish
forever.

Are you relying on your own ability to fix your problems? Does your strength fade quickly?

_____

_____

_____

_____

_____

Talk to God! Ask for God's eternal strength and invincibility from worry.

_____

_____

_____

_____

Psalm 23

What are you worried about today?

_____

_____

_____

_____

You need not want, because the Lord overflows your cup with blessings. You need not fear, because the Lord is with you. You need not worry about where you'll go, because the Lord guides you down the right path. What a blessing this is! Praise be to God that we never have to worry or want for anything!

Psalm 23 is a poem of praise to God! Write down a few examples of his guidance in your life.

_____

_____

_____

_____

Talk to God! Thank God for blessing your life!

_____

_____

_____

_____

DAY 10

1 Peter 5:6-11

What are you worried about today?

_____

_____

_____

_____

Satan loves to use your anxieties to draw you away from God. He fills you with doubt, fear, or disappointment: things that only weaken your mind. God, however, wants the best for you; he wants to strengthen you. You can cast your cares and worries on him, trusting that he has your best interest in mind.

What has Satan used to weaken you? How will you resist Satan and accept God's help?

_____

_____

_____

_____

_____

Talk to God! Ask God to give you the strength to resist Satan's lies.

_____

_____

_____

_____

DAY 11

Hebrews 13:5b-8

What are you worried about today?

_____

_____

_____

_____

God is the omnipotent creator of the earth! If we have an omnipotent Father on our side, what can life throw at us that he can't handle? Not only can God easily handle human struggles, he never changes! He always has and always will care for you.

How do you feel knowing that God's care for you never changes?

_____

_____

_____

_____

_____

Talk to God! Thank God for being steadfast and never changing.

_____

_____

_____

_____

Psalm 56:1-4

What are you worried about today?

_____

_____

_____

_____

Anxiety can often feel overwhelming. It follows you to bed and wakes you up in the morning. It's as if it pursues you. If you trust in God, he will take your anxiety and keep it from following you any longer. You're no longer surrounded by fear, but surrounded by God's comfort and grace.

Has anxiety been surrounding you? How will you distance yourself from your fears and worries?

_____

_____

_____

_____

_____

Talk to God! Ask God to protect you from anxiety and bring you comfort.

_____

_____

_____

_____

DAY 13

1 John 4:16-18

What are you worried about today?

_____

_____

_____

_____

God is love, perfect love. In perfect love there is no fear. As we grow in faith and get know God better, our love for God grows to be more like his love for us: perfect. The more we seek to love God perfectly, the less anxiety and fear control our lives.

How can you grow closer to God? How can you achieve a more perfect love for him?

_____

_____

_____

_____

_____

Talk to God! Thank God for his perfect love and ask him to guide you in your faith walk.

_____

_____

_____

_____

Psalm 97

What are you worried about today?

_____

_____

_____

_____

The Lord promises to rescue and protect us. We need only to love him. It is promised in Psalm 19 that He will show us salvation, honor us, answer our calls, and be with us in times of trouble. Love God, and you will be free from anxiety and receive his promise of blessing.

Yesterday you wrote about how you can love God better. How are you already loving God?

_____

_____

_____

_____

_____

Talk to God! Worship through prayer. Tell him how you love him.

_____

_____

_____

_____

Psalm 61:1-4

What are you worried about today?

_____

_____

_____

_____

In the midst of anxiety, it is easy to forget where
to seek refuge and strength. David was always
quick to cry out to God, not only to seek refuge,
but to praise God for being his refuge and
strength. Take heart in knowing you can find
shelter in God the Father now and forever.

Have you felt as though you need a safe place to hide? Write about how you can find refuge in God.

_____

_____

_____

_____

_____

Talk to God! Worship him for being your safe place!

_____

_____

_____

_____

DAY 16

Zephaniah 3:16-17

What are you worried about today?

_____

_____

_____

_____

Zephaniah 3:16 says "Do not fear. Do not let your hands hang limp." I'm sure you can relate to this limp-handed anxiety. It's the kind that makes your shoulders sag after you throw your hands up in the air and ask God "why?" Take a deep breath, slow down, and listen. He'll soon reach out and show you his plan.

Have you found yourself asking "why" lately? Will you allow God to answer?

_____

_____

_____

_____

_____

Talk to God! Ask him "why" and be ready for his answer!

_____

_____

_____

_____

DAY 17

Psalm 34:17-22

What are you worried about today?

_____

_____

_____

_____

Are you broken-hearted? Do you feel as though anxiety is weighing down your heart? If so, be encouraged! God is close to the broken hearted and saves those who are crushed in spirit. Keep your eyes on God and he will stay close beside you.

Anxiety is weighing you down. How can you remain close to God in times of trouble?

_____

_____

_____

_____

_____

Talk to God! Pray for closeness to God and healing for your broken heart.

_____

_____

_____

_____

DAY 18

1 Samuel 12:20-24

What are you worried about today?

_____

_____

_____

_____

When suffering from anxiety, we often seek out
the help of earthly things. We look to meditation,
exercise, supplements, diets, and doctors. Those
things can be a useful resource, but the true
healing comes from God. Consider all the great
things the Lord has already done for you! He can
handle your anxiety, too!

What do you use to relieve stress and anxiety? How can you seek God's help as well?

_____

_____

_____

_____

_____

Talk to God! Thank the Lord for all he's done and ask him to heal you.

_____

_____

_____

_____

DAY 19

2 Thessalonians 3:16

What are you worried about today?

_____

_____

_____

_____

Imagine you're on the beach of a private island. It's sunny, the air smells fresh, and a gentle breeze rustles the palm leaves. Your anxieties and sufferings in your current life are gone. Peaceful, isn't it? This is exactly the peace that God can bring you. He can bring you perfect peace, you need only to ask and trust him to provide it.

I'm sure you could use the peace of a relaxing vacation. How can you seek peace from God?

_____

_____

_____

_____

_____

Talk to God! Ask God to bring you lasting peace.

_____

_____

_____

_____

DAY 20

Genesis 22:1-14

What are you worried about today?

_____

_____

_____

_____

Obedience, provision, and anxiety are all tied together in Abraham's story. Abraham obeyed God's command and in return, God provided for and blessed Abraham. God is commanding us not to worry, but to trust in him. If we obey and commit our anxieties to him, he will provide and bless us.

Do you need provision and blessing? Which anxieties do you need to let go of?

_____

_____

_____

_____

_____

Talk to God! Pray for God's provision and commit your anxiety to him.

_____

_____

_____

_____

DAY 21

Isaiah 9:6

What are you worried about today?

_____

_____

_____

_____

Jesus has many names. The name I like the most is "Wonderful Counselor." It's hard to be a counselor! Counselors have to relate to their clients' emotions to be successful . Jesus is the most wonderful counselor! He felt the weight of all our anxiety when he bore it on the cross. He knows the heavy weight of worry and, with scripture, counsels you through it!

Where have you experienced Jesus' perfect counseling?

_____

_____

_____

_____

_____

Talk to God! Tell him about your hurts and ask him to provide you counsel.

_____

_____

_____

_____

DAY 22

Psalm 71:1-8

What are you worried about today?

_____

_____

_____

_____

Wow! David wrote such wonderful praise! God is so worthy to be praised. He has been our hope and refuge since the beginning of time. David writes "since birth I have relied on you." God brought you into the world and breathed life into your lungs. Can you not continue to rely on him to sustain you?

What does this passage mean to you? How have we relied on God "since birth?"

_____

_____

_____

_____

_____

Talk to God! Praise him for the life you live and for his constant support.

_____

_____

_____

_____

Romans 15:13

What are you worried about today?

_____

_____

_____

_____

Our God is a God of hope. He'll give us hope if we trust him. Better yet, it's said that we will overflow with hope! Wow, that's a lot of hope. To receive it, you need only to trust God. All your anxieties and worries will be replaced with hope when you trust in the Lord.

What would your life look like if you had overflowing hope?

_____

_____

_____

_____

_____

Talk to God! Put your trust in him and ask him for that overflowing hope!

_____

_____

_____

_____

DAY 24

Romans 8:28-30

What are you worried about today?

_____

_____

_____

_____

God works all things together for the good of those who love him. He called us to be his children and created an individual purpose for every child. All things will work together to complete that purpose. If we love and trust God, our lives will work together for our good. So, leave your anxieties behind! No matter what, God's purpose will be completed.

Where have you seen God work things out for good? Has he revealed his purpose to you?

_____

_____

_____

_____

_____

Talk to God! Ask him to give you a heart of acceptance of your specific purpose.

_____

_____

_____

_____

Mark 4:35-41

What are you worried about today?

_____

_____

_____

_____

The winds were strong, the rain was pouring down. The disciples were caught in a terrifying storm, and they were afraid. Anxiety can often make us feel caught in a storm. We are scared and don't see any blue skies on our horizon. If Jesus calmed the physical storm for the disciples with 2 simple words, he can definitely calm the storm in you.

So you're stuck in a storm of anxiety. What does this storm look like?

_____

_____

_____

_____

_____

Talk to God! Tell him about your storm and ask him to command it to "be still."

_____

_____

_____

_____

DAY 26

Psalm 73:23-28

What are you worried about today?

_____

_____

_____

_____

We are human. We 're anxious, we're fearful, we do not easily trust. These are a few of the many side effects of a sinful nature. God knows that our flesh and humanity cause us to fail. God, however, will never fail. He will pick up our slack when we fall short. He'll give us strength when our sinful nature makes us weak.

How have you fallen short in your anxiety? How has God picked up the slack for you?

_____

_____

_____

_____

_____

Talk to God! Thank him for his strength when your sin makes you weak.

_____

_____

_____

_____

DAY 27

Isaiah 43:1-13

What are you worried about today?

_____

_____

_____

_____

Are you walking through the deep waters of the unknown? God is with you. Are you waist deep in the river called "worry?" God will not let the water sweep over you. Are you surrounded by the raging wildfire of fear? God will not let you be burned. God is your savior! He will keep you from harm.

What dangers are you facing? Do you trust that God will keep them from harming you?

_____

_____

_____

_____

_____

Talk to God! Tell him of the danger that surrounds you and ask for protection.

_____

_____

_____

_____

Isaiah 47:13

What are you worried about today?

_____

_____

_____

_____

A fearful child will often ask, "can you hold my hand?" They're afraid and are looking for the security of someone they trust. God is giving you the same security. He's assuring you that he'll take your hand and walk with you through life's uncertainty and stress.

Write down an instance where you felt God's hand in your anxiety.

_____

_____

_____

_____

_____

Talk to God! Thank him for holding your hand and ask him to never let go.

_____

_____

_____

_____

DAY 29

John 14:1-4

What are you worried about today?

_____

_____

_____

_____

As Christians, we know where we're going. One day, we will be in the presence of our God and our Savior! One day, our anxieties and sufferings will vanish, leaving no trail behind them. We do not need to let our hearts be troubled. We can instead have hope! We'll have hope for the day when we live worry-free with Jesus!

**Do you have hope for an anxiety-free eternity?
Do you believe that promise?**

_____

_____

_____

_____

_____

**Talk to God! Tell him about your
excitement for eternity with him!**

_____

_____

_____

_____

Psalm 116

What are you worried about today?

_____

_____

_____

_____

Reflect on the various ways God has been good to you! Remember the instances when he has delivered you! How did you feel when the Lord came to your rescue? Restful, I hope! When you call on the Lord for help, you will receive rest! Keep your faith strong; soon your suffering will pass and you will receive rest.

What does "rest" look like for you? Write about what helps you relax!

_____

_____

_____

_____

_____

Talk to God! Thank him for giving you rest from life's worries!

_____

_____

_____

_____

Proverbs 31:25-31

What are you worried about today?

_____

_____

_____

_____

The infamous proverbs 31 woman; we all know one and most of us are striving to be one. A proverbs 31 woman wears strength head to toe and has no fear of what's to come. A proverbs 31 woman has relied so heavily on the Lord that her anxiety has been replaced with power. May we all strive to be a proverbs 31 woman!

Imagine you are fearless and strong. What would your life look like?

_____

_____

_____

_____

_____

Talk to God! Ask him to help you become a strong, fearless woman of God!

_____

_____

_____

_____

Let's Connect!

I want to hear from you! I would love feedback about this book, to pray for you, and offer support and comfort.

You can connect with me through my blog: faithfulsoldierswife.com

You can connect with me through email: issy@faithfulsoldierswife.com

You can also connect with me through Instagram:
@issy.menez

Made in the USA
Lexington, KY
22 July 2019